How Do PLANTS GROW?

Published in 2027 by Windmill Books,
an Imprint of Rosen Publishing
2544 Clinton St.
Buffalo, NY 14224

First published in 2018 by Wayland

Managing editor: Victoria Brooker
Creative design: Paul Cherrill

Cataloging-in-Publication Data
Names: Barnham, Kay, author. | Gordon, Mike, illustrator.
Title: How do plants grow? / by Kay Barnham, illustrated by Mike Gordon.
Description: Buffalo, NY : Windmill Books, an imprint of Rosen Publishing, 2027. | Series: Discovering science
Identifiers: ISBN 9781725397163 (pbk.) | ISBN 9781725397170 (library bound) | ISBN 9781725397187 (ebook)
Subjects: LCSH: Plant life cycles--Juvenile literature. | Plants--Juvenile literature. |
Growth (Plants)--Juvenile literature.
Classification: LCC QK731.B345 2027 | DDC 571.82--dc23

Printed in China

CPSIA Compliance Information: Batch #QS27WM
For Further Information contact Rosen Publishing at 1-800-237-9932

DISCOVERING SCIENCE

How Do PLANTS GROW?

Written by
KAY BARNHAM

Illustrated by
MIKE GORDON

WINDMILL BOOKS

"We're going to do something really amazing," Mrs. Wakefield said to the class one morning.

"Are we going on a school trip to the moon?" asked Adam.

The teacher laughed. "Not today," she said. "But we are going to plant our very own seeds."

"What's amazing about that?" said Adam.

"Just wait and see," said Mrs. Wakefield.

"Seeds come in all shapes and sizes,"
said the teacher. She showed them a pea,
an avocado stone, an apple pip, a coffee bean,
a pine cone, a chickpea, and a walnut.

"Are you sure these are all seeds?" asked Adam. "They look so different."

Mrs. Wakefield nodded. "Different types of seeds grow into different plants," she said.

"Look," said Mrs. Wakefield, opening one hand. Striped seeds lay on her palm. "We're going to grow these seeds."

"What are they?" asked Adam's friend, Zayn.

"It's a surprise," said the teacher.
"I hope they're Jack-and-the-beanstalk seeds,"
Zayn whispered.
Adam giggled.

The teacher gave each of the children
a plant pot. They filled them with soil and
Mrs. Wakefield dropped a seed in each one.

Adam sprinkled more soil into his plant pot, so that the seed was hidden. Then he watered it.

"Now, we wait for the seeds to grow," said Mrs. Wakefield.

"How does the seed grow?" asked Adam, peering into his plant pot.

"Inside the seed coat, there is a baby plant," said Mrs. Wakefield. "There's food too."

"When the seed is warm and wet, the plant uses the food to grow. First, roots appear. Then a stem grows. Leaves grow too."

"I wish the plant would hurry up,"
said Adam.

“It’s going to take a few days before the shoot appears,” said Mrs. Wakefield. “So while the seed is growing, let’s think of different sorts of plants.”

“Is a tree a plant?” asked Zayn.
“Yes!” said the teacher. “Let’s go outside and look at some.”

"Some trees are deciduous," said Mrs. Wakefield. "They lose their leaves every autumn and grow new leaves in the spring. Can you name some deciduous trees?"

"Oak trees!" said Adam. "They have huge trunks."
"Apple trees!" said Zayn. "That's where apples grow!"
"Look," said Adam, "their leaves are
different shapes."

"Some trees are evergreen," said the teacher. "Can you guess what that means?"

"Are they always green…?" asked Adam.

"Yes!" said the teacher. "Evergreen trees have green leaves all through the year. Fir trees are evergreens. Trees that grow in rainforests are evergreens too."

The children learned that some plants grow in the wild. "Daisies, dandelions, and buttercups are wildflowers," said the teacher. "They grow where the conditions are right for them."

"Who looks after them?" asked Adam.
"No one," said the teacher.
"They don't need any care at all."

The teacher explained that plants
in gardens often come from somewhere else.
"Garden plants need to be looked after," she said.

"For example, if they come from a hot country and
they are planted in a cold country, then
they need to be kept warm in a greenhouse."

After school, Adam and his mom went to their community garden. Plants grew in neat rows. "What are these?" asked Adam.

"I'm growing onions, carrots, and potatoes for dinner," Mom said, pointing to them. "And I'm growing strawberries for dessert!"

“This is better than a grocery store,” said Adam.
“It’s a lot cheaper!” Mom laughed.

At school, a green shoot appeared in Adam's plant pot. "Hurray!" he said. "At last!" The children's plants grew taller and taller and taller. Soon, they were taller than the children. Leaves grew.

At the top of each plant, petals
opened and a flower appeared.
"Now do you know what these plants are?"
asked Mrs. Wakefield.
"Sunflowers!" chorused the pupils.

“This flower is nearly as big as my head!”
said Adam, and everyone laughed.
Mrs. Wakefield pointed to the middle
of Adam’s flower.

“Look, there are hundreds of sunflower seeds,” she said. “If we plant them, new sunflowers will grow!”

“Wow,” said Adam. “Plants really are amazing.”

NOTES FOR PARENTS AND TEACHERS

The aim of this book is to introduce children to scientific concepts in an entertaining, informative way. Here are some ideas for activities that will encourage them to think further about plants – and have fun doing it!

ACTIVITIES

1. Go on a nature walk with your class. Count how many different plants you can find. Look out for deciduous and evergreen trees!

2. Cut out plant pictures from magazines and make a plant collage. Include flowers, trees, shrubs, and plants from all over the world.

3. Can you rearrange these anagrams to find five phrases to do with plants?

ICED DUO US

SWIRLED WOLF

OATS POET

NEWS FLOUR

RAG NED

DECIDUOUS, WILDFLOWERS, POTATOES, SUNFLOWER, GARDEN

GROW YOUR OWN SUNFLOWER!

Put a few pebbles at the bottom of a plant pot. Fill the pot nearly to the top with soil. Then drop a sunflower seed on top, and add a little more soil.

Put the plant pot in a sunny place. Remember to water your sunflower every day. After a few days, a shoot will appear!

As your sunflower grows taller, tie the stem to a stick or a cane. This will stop it from falling over.

DID YOU KNOW ...?

The tallest tree in the world is a giant redwood, somewhere in California. It is nearly 545 feet (116 m) tall. To keep it safe, only a few people know exactly where it is . . .

Some plants eat meat! A Venus flytrap is a plant that eats flies and other small insects.

There are about 400,000 different types of plants in the world.

BOOKS TO SHARE

Plants
(*Boom Science* series)
by Georgia Amson-Bradshaw
(Wayland, 2018)

Seed Safari
(*Plant Life* series)
by Judith Heneghan
(Wayland, 2018)

The Amazing Life Cycle of Plants
(*Look and Wonder* series)
by Kay Barnham
(Wayland, 2018)

Plants
(*The Curiosity Box* series)
by Peter Riley
(Watts Publishing, 2016)